CELEBRATING Water

story by
Aaron William Perry

art by
Yvonne Kozlina

Celebrating Water

Copyright © 2021 Aaron William Perry

All rights reserved. No part of this book may be reproduced in any form or by any electronic or mechanical means, including information storage and retrieval systems, without permission in writing from the publisher, except by reviewers, who may quote brief passages in a review.

ISBN: 978-1-7347229-4-9 (paperbacl)
ISBN: 978-1-7347229-5-6 (ebook)

Library of Congress Control Number: applied for

Earth Water Press, Denver Colorado
www.earthwaterpress.com

To book this author for a speaking engagement or workshop, contact engage@yonearth.org

Printed in the United States of America

Hi Friends!

My name is Sophia, and I'm a honey bee. I love flowers, sunshine and rainbows. I'm so excited to join you on this adventure Celebrating Water! Look for me in each picture: I'll be your friend and guide through the whole book!

We may encounter some new terms and concepts. Not to worry! The Y on Earth Community team has provided us resources at the back of the book, including a key word list for the bold, italicized words in the story, to help answer questions and share some special knowledge and inspiration with you!

Are you ready for an adventure together?

Buzzing with Love,

Brother and Sister love to take hikes with their mom and dad.

One day, they drove for three hours from their home in New York City and went on a hike to the Great Waterfall.

The Great Waterfall is **sacred** to the **Indigenous** people of that land in Upstate New York, the *Kanien´kehá:ka* people, who are also known as the Mohawk Nation. They are the eastern most members of the *Haudenosaunee*, the *"People of the Long House"* also known as the great **Iroquois Confederacy**.

Sister and Brother stood before the Great Waterfall in awe of the power, magic, and beauty of it. Brother saw **rainbows** throughout the rising mists, Sister heard singing voices in the roar of the falling water, and they could both feel and smell the mist in the air.

At the Waterfall they met one of the Tribal Elders, who told them this waterfall is the sacred gateway to the East, and is called *She Who Speaks Loudly*. The Elder told the children, "If you quiet your mind and listen with your heart, you may hear her special message."

He sang them ancient water songs and told them why water is so sacred to the people of Earth.

He lit a **ceremonial** fire, and this is what he said:

"In the days of our ancestors, everybody celebrated water. They knew that the sacred rains fall from the heavens, **_nourishing_** all of us: the land, the soil, the insects, the animals, the ferns, the trees, and the people. It soaks into the soil and germinates the seeds, singing them sweet growing songs. Most people have forgotten to listen to these songs. But some of us still remember, and sit very still in the woods to hear them. Can you hear the songs?"

The Wise Elder continued "The rains nourish the plants and they grow up, up, up toward the sun. The sunlight and water combine with the wind and the magical life of the soil to give the plants everything that they need to grow and blossom. The sunflower is one of my favorites, for the flowers follow the path of the sun – they are what's called **heliotropic**. That's why they're called the flower of the sun. When it's really cloudy, instead of looking at the sun, the sunflowers look at their neighbors, nourished by the abundant, golden light and beauty of one another. Have you ever seen sunflowers looking at each other on a cloudy day?"

"In time they are pollinated by the bees, butterflies, birds, and other pollinators, and grow seeds that drop to the ground. The seeds rest in the soil, patiently awaiting the spring rains that wake them up and invite them to grow as new baby plants. Thus the cycle repeats itself again and again. This is the great circle of life."

"But, it's not just flowering plants that the water nourishes – it's all of life on Earth! This includes you, Brother and Sister, and all of your friends, family, and every single human being on the planet. You see, you need to drink clean, pure water every day in order to stay healthy, to feel good, and to succeed in life. Water is essential to everything we do."

"And…" continued the Wise Elder, "Did you know that your body is at least 72% water? Do you know what **per cent** means? It means out of one hundred – thus, if something is 72% water, that means that out of every 100 pounds, 72 of those pounds are water! How many pounds of water do you each have? All living creatures on the planet – plants, animals, even bees – are made up mostly of water. Isn't that amazing!?"

"In fact, the entire Earth is covered in about 72% water. Can you believe it? We live on land, but most of our planet is a watery world, with rivers, lakes, and a deep, deep ocean enveloping the land. Have you ever seen the ocean? It's breathtaking in its size and beauty, and is so majestic. The ocean is magnificent, and is a very important part of our sacred planet. The sun ***evaporates*** water from the ocean, making clouds. Those clouds float over the land and mountains and drop the water in rain, and sometimes snow."

"Have you ever looked closely at a snowflake? The **geometry** of each snowflake is a unique, six-sided or **hexagonal** shape. The geometry of water is very special, and contains many sacred angles and structures hidden within its fluid forms. Our ancestors told us that water carries the **memory** and wisdom of the land and the people, and sings a living song within each of us. Science is just now becoming **sophisticated** enough to consider such subtle and sublime possibilities. Can you see the hexagonal geometry? Can you draw your own unique snowflake?"

"When it freezes, water becomes a solid that is less dense than the water, therefore floating on top. Of course, many animals like the Polar Bear rely on ice to travel and rest when they're not swimming. Have you ever seen an iceberg in the water? How about a *glacier* in the mountains? Have you seen ice cubes floating in your own glass of water? One of the most mysterious substances on the planet, water has physical properties unlike any other substance – some would say it is magical in its ways."

Brother and Sister told the Tribal Elder about the time they went snorkeling in the ocean and saw an amazing diversity of creatures. Animals, plants, and corals of stunning, vivid colors were cohabitating in the salt water, each one playing a special role in the great **web of life**.

However, they were saddened to discover an overwhelming mess of **pollution** choking out these habitats. From soaps and detergents being washed down bathroom drains, to **toxic** petroleum and pesticide spills flowing into the ocean from factories and non-organic agricultural fields, a terrible concoction of chemical pollution swirled about discarded plastic, metal, and rubber trash. It made Brother and Sister cry with sorrow.

But they were even sadder when they came across a dead **orca** that had been killed by all of the trash and pollution. And, a little further down the beach they found a sea turtle so twisted up in nylon rope that it couldn't get back to the water or swim away.

Brother and Sister knew they had to help, and set about cutting the turtle loose as quickly as possible. The ocean and her creatures really need our help – will you help them too? What can you do to help?

A few days later, Mother and Father took Sister and Brother to the mineral hot springs so that they could be nourished and ***rejuvenated*** by the natural pools. Brother and Sister love soaking in the water, and when they aren't at the natural hot springs, they soak in special mineral salt baths in their tub right at home.

Water is the wellspring of all life, and nourishes us in so many ways.

Do you like to soak and swim in the water?

Earth is a sacred living being, with magical, living water animating all life. She needs our help, and especially needs us to help clean up pollution and toxicity so that we restore the pristine nature of this majestic planet.

Will you help?

Will you help Brother and Sister in this important work?

Will you help to teach others to celebrate water too?

The End

About the Y on Earth Community

The Y on Earth Community is a growing movement of students, parents, teachers, entrepreneurs, executives, and organizational leaders helping to mobilize stewardship and sustainability throughout our culture.

We provide powerful, accessible tools and hope-filled inspiration to enhance day-to-day health and well being while deeply aligning with global strategies for regeneration, stewardship, and sustainability. Our simple and empowering tools for "Thriving"—in the domains of soil, gardens, food, nature, and stewardship—are fun for children of all ages!

You will find additional children's books, videos, resources, and activity guides at yonearth.org. Be sure to check out our Stewardship & Sustainability Podcast series on the website as well!

SPONSORS

We would like to say a special "thank you" to our partners and affiliate sponsors! Through our Y on Earth Approved ecosystem, you can get exclusive deals and discounts from these great companies at yonearth.org/partners-supporters:

  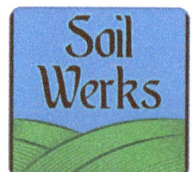   

Calls To Action

You can help Sister and Brother and thousands of other people all around the world, as we take better care of the water. We can all make choices and take action to detoxify the water, to clean up pollution, and to experience and celebrate the majestic, magical qualities of water! Here are several things you can do to help:

1. Eliminate toxic chemicals like pesticides and herbicides from your garden and yard.

2. Use organic and non-toxic dish soap, laundry detergent, bath soaps, shampoos, conditioners, and cleaning products in your home and school.

3. Sit quietly by water (a lake, a river, or a babbling brook), and listen to the water's sacred song.

4. Buy and eat organic, biodynamic, and regenerative food and beverage products whenever possible.

5. Create water color art together.

6. Draw, paint, and cut-out snowflakes.

7. Share a biodynamic water stir ceremony (see yonearth.org/soil-activation for videos and information).

8. Where does your water come from? Draw a map of your watershed.

9. Engage with the Y on Earth Community for further information, inspiration, and action items!

Ocean Conservancy

Ocean Conservancy is working with you to protect the ocean from today's greatest global challenges. Together, we create science-based solutions for a healthy ocean and the wildlife and communities that depend on it. (oceanconservancy.org)

Sea Shepherd

Sea Shepherd works to end the destruction of habitat and slaughter of wildlife in the world's oceans in order to conserve and protect ecosystems and species. (seashepherd.org)

KEY WORD LIST

Ceremonial: deliberate, intentional, and reverential; describing practices and rituals of spiritual or religious significance in cultures throughout the world.

Evaporate: to transform matter from a liquid to a gaseous state.

Geometry: the study and practice of shapes, forms, spatial relationships, and patterns, from the Greek words Geo (meaning "Earth") and Meter (meaning "measure").

Glacier: compacted ice and snow that accumulates over hundreds and thousands of years.

Heliotropic: following the sun, from the Greek Helios (meaning "sun") and Tropos (meaning "to move").

Hexagonal: six-sided, from the Greek Hexa (meaning "six") and Gon (meaning "side").

Indigenous: belonging to, native to, from, part of, and in deep relationship to a particular ecosystem, environment, or place on Earth.

Iroquois Confederacy: an alliance of six Native American tribes, the Mohawk, Onondaga, Oneida, Cayuga, Seneca and Tuscarora, who established one of the earliest forms of democracy in the world, and inspired the Framers of the United States Constitution, especially Benjamin Franklin.

Memory: the recording, storing, embedding, imprinting and ability to recall information, knowledge, and wisdom.

Nourishing: caring for, providing sustenance, stewarding, loving, invigorating, and vitalizing.

Orca: an air breathing mammal of the sea and member of the whale family, sacred to many Indigenous people.

Per Cent: the portion or ratio of a numeric value compared to one hundred.

Pollinators: bees, butterflies, birds, bats, and other animals and insects that carry pollen from the male anther of one flower to the female stigma of another, thus engendering the fertility cycle of reproduction to create more plants.

Pollution: something discharged and accumulated that is harmful, unhealthy, or poisonous.

Rainbow: a colorful prism of refraction created by the interaction of light and water or other translucent material.

Rejuvenate: to make young again, to restore, to imbue with health and wellness.

Sacred: deserving of special respect and reverence, and understood to carry special significance.

Sophisticated: knowledgeable, complex in its understanding, appropriately advanced, learned or educated.

Toxic: causing damage to living tissues, organisms, and ecosystems.

Web of life: the complex system of interconnected relationships between living organisms making up the sacred biosphere of planet Earth.

ACKNOWLEDGEMENTS

It takes a whole village to create and publish these children's books! Yvonne and Aaron wish to say "Thank you" to the following people who generously shared their knowledge, time, and expertise, who supported the project, and who helped make *Celebrating Water* come alive ~ including some very special thought leaders from bygone times.

Al & Christina Stemp	Leonardo Da Vinci
Artem Nikulkov	Kimba Arem
Bethany Yarrow	Maggie McLaughlin
Brad & Lindsay Lidge	Marissa Pulaski
Caressa Ayres	Nick DiDomenico
Charmaine Boudreaux	Roger Jock
Jack Dawson	Viktor Schauberger
Katie Garces	

We wish to say a very special "Thank you" to Caressa, Charmaine, and Jack for your editorial feedback on the story, and to Maggie for designing and assembling such a beautiful book to share with all of our friends!

About the Author

Author and founder of the Y on Earth Community, Aaron William Perry is an entrepreneur, writer, speaker, consultant, and father. The author of *Y on Earth: Get Smarter, Feel Better, Heal the Planet,* Aaron works with the Y on Earth Community and Impact Ambassadors to spread the THRIVING and SUSTAINABILITY messages of hopeful and empowering information and inspiration to diverse communities throughout the world. He resides in Colorado where he loves to hike in the mountains, is continually in awe of the ever-changing weather, and entertained by the hilarious antics of his backyard, free-range (and free-thinking) chickens.

About the Illustrator

Yvonne Kozlina is a professional portrait artist and painter who originally hails from Pittsburgh, Pennsylvania and now makes Colorado her home. A mother and grandmother, She loves children and has taught art to diverse children of all ages. Yvonne's photo-realistic style is uncanny, as she taps in to the essence of the people she paints and draws. She is also an avid animal lover, gardener, and enjoys taking walks through the neighborhood when she isn't at her easel painting. See Yvonne's artwork and learn more about her custom portrait services at yvonnekozlina.com.

Ciao for now!

www.ingramcontent.com/pod-product-compliance
Lightning Source LLC
Chambersburg PA
CBHW042355070526
44585CB00028B/2938